The Competitive Senior Golfer

The Competitive Senior Golfer

Brian Waites

CASTLE
publications

Castle Publications
A Division of Nottingham University Press
Manor Farm, Main Street
Thrumpton, Nottingham, NG11 0AX, UK

NOTTINGHAM

First published 1997
© B Waites

British Library Cataloguing in Publication Data
A catalogue record for this book is available from the British Library

ISBN 1-897676-62X

Typeset by Castle Publications, Nottingham
Printed and bound by Redwood Books, Trowbridge, Wiltshire

INTRODUCTION

My career on the European Tour covered some 28 years. My career on the Senior Tour almost ended after 18 months.

   As many of you know, I had a rather serious car accident early one morning when travelling to a Pro Am at Fulford Golf Club. After a month in intensive care and 4 months in hospital, I began to wonder if I would ever play golf again. It's not a nice thought even for someone who is a club golfer let alone someone who plays golf for a living.

Professional golfers fall into three categories. The ones who teach, the ones who are good shop keepers and the ones who can make money playing the game. Although there is some overlap, there are these three categories and I had to decide which one to take for the future.

I think all professionals start with wanting to be in the latter group and it didn't take me long to decide that I wanted to stay there. Golf was calling me back. I needed to feel the pressure of competition, the pleasure of the fairway splitting drive, the putt to win- need I go on? You know how I felt.

I had to take full advantage of the physiotherapy and get fit. My friends were telling me to take a holiday and get some colour back in my face, but that would only delay things. I would take a holiday when the physio told me there was nothing more that she could do for me. Determination has always been one of my strong points and, 9 months after the accident, I was back on Tour. I did not play in all of the events in my first year back, but after the second year I finished 4th in the order of merit.

The object of this book is to encourage all senior golfers to hang in there. When we become seniors it does not mean that we are no longer competitive. We must make use of our assets, particularly the one that the younger players just do not have, and that is experience. We have to make use of our knowledge of course management and maximise on our ability, make use of modern technology, by using the most suitable clubs, shafts and balls, and adjust our method to suit our seniority. This way we will be able to play this great game of ours forever.

There are of course many golfers who do not start to play golf until their families have "flown the nest" and they too need to realise that they will still be able to compete. Older beginners need to be taught and encouraged, and experienced golfers need encouragement and reference facilities for fault finding. I do hope that my book provides these requirements.

Age is not a problem in golf as many of you will accept if you follow the golf tours. Being able to compete with younger players on the professional tours may be difficult for the older pro but in the amateur game handicaps overcome many of the problems. As we become older we can remain competitive through the pleasure of playing and less from the overwhelming urge to win which motivates many young players. Having said that, we all play to win and have to find the best ways to achieve it.

CONTENTS

I would like to thank Dennis Vardy for his invaluable help in
putting this book together.

Photographs courtesy of Today's Golfer Magazine and Steve Tristram.

ONE

Practice Makes Perfect

Unfortunately, practise is one part of the game for which the senior club golfer finds little time. Most of them do not practise at all except for the occasional visit to the putting green. It does seem strange that practise time should reduce as the years roll on, because nothing else seems to change. They still have their enthusiasm to play. The pleasures and the friendships also remain the same, so why not the practise? I know that there is an old saying, "You can't teach an old dog new tricks" but we are golfers and our competitive edge must be kept sharp. We must keep repeating our personal swing method to keep it in good order. If we don't then we lose consistency, handicaps increase and the game becomes little more than a walk in the fresh air.

Some golfers trust to luck every time they play. They should question their objectives and ask themselves what they want from the game. Maybe if they knew how to practise and enjoyed doing so, they would become more competent and their handicaps would stop going up. A low figure handicap is something to be proud of as we get older, in fact, at my club a gentleman of 73 recently reduced his handicap from 13 to 12. He is now running about like a two year old and telling everyone shot by shot how he did it. To me, pride in performance is everything and I practise with that in mind.

My practise routine has changed very little over the years. There was a change for a while after my accident when I spent more than my usual amount of time playing shots from the rough. Practising this way was to bring a bit of strength back into my hands and arms and in particular my right wrist. This practise has been of great benefit to me and the same experience would benefit all golfers. You will not only improve your ability to recover from a bad lie, you will also find out how far you can hit the ball from the rough and understand that you should loosen your grip and not tighten it. This is a shot where club head speed is of paramount importance. To tighten your grip will reduce wrist action and make you try to swing quicker. Neither of these things will help you to play the shot.

Practise is not just a habit to get into, it has to be enjoyed. To enjoy anything there must be reward and this is where some golfers fail in their practise. They only go to the range to iron out a fault and generally they practise that fault.

Practise has to follow a logical pattern. It is not about hitting lots and lots of golf balls it's about hitting good golf shots. Some golfers use the hit and miss method of training where they hit balls until they get one right and think that they have solved their problem. You have to take a lesson to find where your swing is failing and then set about to correct the fault.

Swing faults creep into your game as you play and are practised until you realise that you can no longer tolerate them. You then have to follow a "Cure" routine to clear yourself of the problem. Of course these are intermittent faults and have nothing to do with your individual swing method.

Practise is not solely to cure faults. At all levels of the game we have to keep reminding our golfing muscles how we would like them to work. The coordination of body movements is very precise. I practise daily to keep my golf machine in order, so do all other dedicated professionals. I have to ask that if talented golfers need to practise on a regular basis, how do less talented players expect to have any semblance of consistency without regular practise? Without consistency, confidence is very hard to find.

There is a big difference between learning how to play golf and practising golf. Learning how to play by following basic routines of grip stance and swing are quite well known and vary only slightly depending on the teacher.

This type of practise range work takes time and mental effort. Perhaps the main advice for the beginner is that the length of time spent at this work is important. Some beginners and some experienced golfers for that matter, stay at practise for too long. Their interest and enthusiasm keeps them there and can actually be their worst enemy.

You will already know that sore hands can result from spending too long a period of time hitting golf balls, but there is a much more serious reason for short period practise. Sore hands and aching muscles and loss of concentration inhibit learning. Your ability to concentrate will reduce as time goes on and this can have a serious effect on your ability to learn. You will have to find out where this fall off in your powers of attention start to fail because this is when you must stop. If you carry on you will hit more bad shots than good and ruin the earlier good work.

Some golfers can practise for longer periods of time than others. On average I would say that 40 balls are quite enough at one spell. If you have the time to hit more, the drill is to break off at this time and either pick up the used balls or rest with a coffee for 15 minutes or so. Then you can start afresh with your ability to concentrate restored.

Practise for the experienced golfer must follow a similar time pattern with a different and more intense routine. It's no good believing that a peaceful practise environment will develop a swing to stand up to the pressure of competition. The two conditions are poles apart and a routine for learning to play or solving swing problems are not a satisfactory system to prepare for competitive golf.

Competition pressure demands pressure practise and perhaps you could benefit from the training methods which I used as a young professional.

I never went down to the practise range if no one else was there. We do not play golf under such conditions. I always preferred to practise whilst being watched by a member of the club. This way I was always required to concentrate on each shot. I also enjoyed demonstrating how to recover from divot holes etc.

The course where all this took place is Hesketh Golf Club and their practise ground had an added benefit. Just in front of the tee area there was a bramble thicket, hit the ball in there and it's difficult to reach, never mind find. This facility really does make you attend to your business. It's the same when you explain and demonstrate the difference in flight and distance when playing from a good and bad lie. For your own good, use this type of practise as often as you can.

If you analyse each game you play and calculate the different lies you encounter, you can then section your practise routine to suit. If your average score is 90, then tee shots with woods amount to only 14 on a standard layout. If you are a reasonable putter may be you average 30 putts, so almost half of your shots are fairway shots. Some shots will be played with woods and some with irons. From these different types of shot which constitute a round of golf you have to schedule your practise sessions.

The logical way to organize practise is to decide where you drop the most of your shots. It could be that you are a bad bunker player and if so, get some practise. Gary Player will be seen practising bunker shots at every senior event, and he's the world's best at this shot. When the pressure of competition is on, Gary can always go for the most

Figure 1 Gary Player is a very kind and caring man.

difficult of flag positions because he knows that if he does go in the bunker, he will get up and down. Incidentally, only a few hours after my accident Gary rang the hospital from half way round the world. He's not just a great golfer, he's a very kind and caring man.

In a round of golf you will spend a large amount of time on and around the greens. If you are a good putter then the same Gary Player theory applies. If you do miss a green then you can save par by putting well and this again has a knock on effect. If you are a confident putter then the pressure is taken off those chips and pitches, which in turn takes pressure off your approach work. I hope that you are following my philosophy.

If you have to decide which part of golf is the most important, then it has to be putting - an area of golf where age and strength of arm play little part. In fact, it is true to say that after technique, experience is the most important element in good putting.

Another thing we can establish on the practise ground is how far we hit the ball with each club. I'll tell you now, it's not as far as your wishful thinking expects. Even then, distances change according to the weather and to the type of grass. We all know that we have to account for wind and temperature but the type of grass on a course will also change distances.

Figure 2 Royal Birkdale is one of the best seaside courses.

On a seaside course the ball will sit tight to the ground and the impact point on the club will be low on the clubface. This will give the ball more spin than a ball which impacts higher up on the face. When playing from lies on lush grass both the higher impact point and the interference of grass being trapped between the ball and the club will reduce the backspin.

The next time you play, take note of how many times you play short. If you do get up to the green, how many times are you short of the flag?

Many amateurs rely on the ball running up to the green. This is OK if you need the extra distance, but why play a seven iron to run up when you could play a six iron and land on the green. This is how the pro would play the shot to avoid those left and right kicks which sometimes put good shots in bunkers. I find that many amateurs would play a particular iron shot and then complain when it came up short. Some golfers do like to boast about being big hitters even if they are not, and this only adds to their score.

Yardages are not always easy to calculate and for this reason it is not always good to "eye ball" a distance. These days we have yardage charts and 150 yard markers from the greens to help make your decisions over club selection. Even so, we all know that visits to see an optician for eye sight tests come around quite frequently and we should take them.

You have to be able to focus on the ball to achieve good stance and set-up and if you have difficulty seeing your target you are at a real disadvantage. Club selection is vital at all levels of the game. Please make sure that you are properly equipped to do the job.

Practising to play golf has to be organised to achieve consistency. There is no other good reason for being there, so get it right and you will find the time rewarding.

TWO

As we all get older, and particularly if we have a health problem, our golf swing will change. For instance it will almost certainly become shorter because of an increasing waist measurement, but it does not mean that we will not hit the ball as far. Some golfers have never had a long backswing. Take the American - Doug Sanders - his backswing is so short that he almost doesn't have one. In fact for many senior golfers a shorter backswing could be an advantage and not a disadvantage.

Physically the game of golf may seem quite demanding. Difficulties could be found from the twisting motion of the body. Then there is the necessity for good balance and the strength of leg to walk for miles. Fortunately it is not as difficult as it seems at first glance. The game is within reasonable reach for all of those who wish to play. Age, and a not too perfect body is not a set back if we take a sensible look at the changes we have to make as we get older.

Some golfers may find the strength of leg and general fitness could be improved, but one physical thing we must all understand from the very beginning is that we are all built differently. For this reason we all swing the club in different ways and good advice for one is not always good for another.

Let me take just one example to make my point. When I address the ball, I prefer to have my weight on the balls of my feet. This gives me better manoeuvrability in my legs. Other golfers I know like to have their weight further back towards their heels. Maybe this is because they do not have the same sense of balance as I do, but what ever the reason the distance that we stand away from the ball differs.

There are so many reasons why we all swing differently, although some differences are only very slight. Having established this we can go on to ask, " Is it necessary to have a classical swing?"

Well, some people certainly say so. Many of the all time greats had - and have - good swings: Ben Hogan, Sam Snead, Henry Cotton; so it could be an advantage. But what about people like Arnold Palmer, Hubert Green and Calvin Peete? They all found stardom, so we must say that if your swing produces good results and you can repeat it when the pressure is on, then it's good enough. Even if it does not look text book quality, at the end of the day the lowest score wins.

"Individual" swings do work. My own for example - far too fast some people say. Well, it doesn't seem fast to me, I feel it takes no longer than the average golfer.

The speed of your swing depends mainly on the type of person you are. I am a busy person; I like to get on with things. I walk quickly (perhaps a little slower now because of my right knee) and I would much prefer a round of golf to take no more than three hours.

Figure 3   Arnold Palmer - great golfer - great swing.

There are others on the Tour who do take more time over shot making than I do. Some of them need a kick up the back side, but generally it does not increase overall time because they are not hitting the ball all that often. Unfortunately some amateurs think that it will improve their game if they take the same amount of time to play a shot; this can extend medal rounds into long days. It is not good for the game to be slow and certainly no good if you have to wait behind a slow group. Very often these days a game can be more of a trial in patience than trying to card the lowest score.

Nick Faldo has a swing which is much slower than mine and I would say that it does not seem slow to him as mine does not seem fast to me. It is his method, his speed; he cannot change and neither should you change from your natural rhythm.

Another example is Eamon Darcy. Here is an individual swing, if you like, and one which would be difficult to copy. However it works to a very high standard. His swing may seem a little odd going back and at the top, but in the hitting area it does the correct things. It has to, to provide the results.

Everyone's personal method gives him a quality within his game for which he becomes renowned. Mine is consistency of strike. When I hit a ball, under ideal conditions, I know to within a couple of feet how far it will go with any club in the bag. Of course things like a gusting wind and hard ground can make judgement of distances difficult on occasions, but as a rule my distance is quite consistent.

Lee Trevino's natural shot is a controlled fade shot. He misses very few fairways or short hole greens which makes him a very formidable opponent. If you can keep the ball on the short grass it makes golf so much easier, as Lee shows, and the easier we make it for ourselves, the more we are likely to laugh and joke like Lee does.

Coming back to Eamon, I am sure you have noticed his little "cut up" shots around the green. He is absolutely superb at these delicate little shots from having a natural across the line swing.

One of the main ingredients of any good swing is good balance, and we must understand that the point on the club face at which the ball must make contact is quite small. To line the ball up with this point at address is one thing; to raise the club to the top of the backswing and return it to the same position is another, requiring a very good sense of balance.

Every time we play we see players hit the ball from the toe or heel of the club, and we all do it more often than we would like. Why does it happen? Well, it's obvious isn't it? Sometime during the swing we have changed our position relative to the ball.

From our address we move position. Perhaps because of the failure to understand that the swing is a pivot action, or just as likely through a failure to retain proper balance. It may be easier to put more emphasis on the need for good balance if we look at the main object of the game.

Figure 4 Of all the very pleasant golf courses I have played over the years, Silloth on Solway rates very highly. Those of you who enjoy playing classic links golf courses will find Silloth one of the best.

We are expected to hit a ball, 1.68 inches in diameter and weighing a mere 1.62 ounces, from point A to point B over very pleasant countryside. To do this we have what is called a clubhead, fashioned to fit a shaft. These clubheads are made from all sorts of materials: wood, steel, plastic, brass, beryllium copper and many more.

Whereas the shaft is attached to the heel of the head in irons and woods, this is not necessarily so for putters. This conforms with the rules of golf set down by the Royal and Ancient Club of St Andrews, the game's governing body. Putters, by the way, can have the shaft positioned anywhere along it's length, the main rule being that the length of the putter head must be greater than it's width.

It may appear to the beginner that a ball struck anywhere on the face of the clubhead would do the job quite well. It may also seem logical that as the clubhead sticks out from the side of the shaft, it will always have a tendency to twist in the hands when we hit the ball. Neither of these is true.

All clubs have what is called a sweet spot, a spot where if the ball connects the twist will be reduced to a minimum. It is also the point where maximum force is exerted on the ball. One way you will notice this is because very little force is transmitted back to your hands. We all know the shot, it feels so good.

You can find where this spot is on all of your clubs quite easily. Take a club and hold it as in figure 5. If you now tap the face with a tee peg at different places along it's length, you will soon find the place where there is no twist of the face. (It is important that you do this with your putter and mark its position. It may not be where the manufacturer has placed the mark.)

Figure 5 Checking the sweet spot.

Good balance is an essential ingredient of quality golf. Just watch a good golfer and see how he finishes his swing after playing a good shot. He will be in a statue-like pose, perfectly still to watch and enjoy the results of his efforts.

I have been in the game for some very enjoyable years and seen some quite varied interpretations of the swing, some good and some bad. I have now come to the conclusion that the classical swing does not seem too important and that we should work to develop the swing which suits our own physical ability.

THREE

Different ways to hold a club

The game of golf has set rules to which we must all adhere. Sometimes they get broken, but not always knowingly and golfers question or discuss them almost every time they play.

Apart from the rules of golf can at times need explaining to even the most experienced of players. They can be misinterpreted and all golfers should seek the advice of their match secretary to settle any uncertainty surrounding a rule. For instance a free drop on the green is not a drop, you must place the ball.

Apart from the rules, there are other set and correct procedures which we must adhere to and they are related to the way we apply ourselves to the game, both mentally and physically.

Even if we accept that all golfers will swing the club differently through their own individual "make up", there are certain methods and habits to which we must all conform.

The way we hold the club is one example and this is known as "The grip". There are three conventional ways of doing this and whichever one we choose, we must use it correctly. All three are very good and tried methods, and if you do have a variation on these I advise you to get out of the habit and conform to the original. Each of them has stood the test of time and are used by good players. I personally do not know of a good player with a funny grip.

The three grips are:

The Vardon Grip - figure 6

The Interlocking Grip - figure 7

The Baseball Grip (the two handed grip) - figure 8

The grip should be made in the order shown in figure 9, with the club held in the fingers and not the palms of the hands. Some golfers find this advice difficult to follow and perhaps better advice would be, "Ideally the club should be held in the fingers", because this is advice for the strong golfer who usually makes the professional ranks. Some golfers have short fingers and would find it impossible, so the one that suits you is the best.

Figure 6 The Vardon Grip.

Figure 7 The Interlocking Grip.

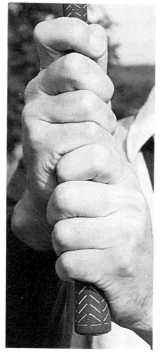

Figure 8 The Baseball Grip.

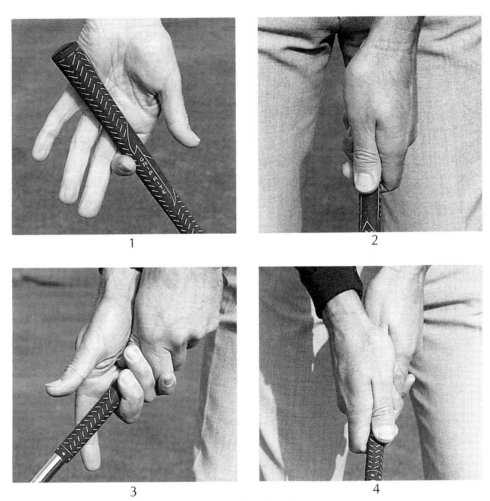

Figure 9 The grip order.

The Vardon grip, first used by the great man himself, is the most commonly used. Vardon found that the grip was made more effective if the right hand was moved nearer to the left by overlapping the little finger of the right hand over the forefinger of the left hand. This gives more freedom of movement. The wrists being closer together allows them to work more effectively without restricting the bending and twisting. In effect, they work better as one unit. A weakening of the right hand does take place to balance out the extra strength which most people have in their right hand. Of course not all people have a dominant right hand and perhaps one of the other grips would be more suited to them.

The interlocking grip has a similar left hand position on the club but the little finger of the right hand interlocks with the forefinger of the left hand.

The Baseball grip, as its name suggests, has all the fingers of both hands in contact with the club. The "V's" made between the forefinger and the thumb must point to a position half way between the right shoulder and the neck, as in the other two grips.

This is the grip that many golfers take up as the years progress. As our strength of grip gets less, having two full hands on the club does help. Another way which may help those whose fingers get a little stiff particularly in the mornings or towards the end of a round of golf, is to use a larger diameter grip. These are made by a number of manufacturers and your pro will be able to advise you which one would be best for your needs.

There is something which some beginners fail to grasp and consequently many of them never become very good at the game. This is concerning the position of the hands at any time during the swing. They are always in line with the club face (figure 10). If it were possible to open your hands at the top of the backswing, then you would see the back of your left hand and the front of your right hand are parallel to the plane of the club face. Check your hand position at the address. The left hand and right hand positions will be aligned this way if you have gripped the club correctly. They must be returned to this position of alignment at the point of impact.

Some golfers fail to follow this basic requirement and therefore develop the wrong type of hand action. Their grip is changed to compensate for an error in wrist action and this results in some grips looking as if they belong more in a horror movie than on a golf course.

There are only two slight variations to use when our game is slightly off. On some days we find that we hit the ball a little right or a little left of our target. Perhaps we are fading the ball or have for some unknown reason found the draw of which we have always been seeking. Whichever, we may need to make an "emergency" change to compensate for the error of line.

We may need to use a stronger grip (figure 11). We achieve this by placing the left hand more on top of the club and the right hand more underneath. This is used to bring the face to square if it was staying open.

The other variation will prevent the club returning closed at impact position and this means moving the hands the other way. The left hand will be more underneath and the right more on the top (figure 12).

It is vitally important to conform with respect to how we hold the club, because without this we will not have the means to manoeuvre the ball in any direction. There are times in every game when a player has to move the ball in flight either to the left or to the right. The position of the trees often determines this, but it's more likely that a player will play his ball into a "blind" position and be unable to see the flag. You cannot slice with a grip designed to hook, or move one the other way with a weakgrip. Some will say, "I can," and my advice to them is see a good pro. for a lesson and get that wrist action sorted out.

Conventional grips are quite straightforward. First hold a club in the left hand, and then place the right hand as in figure 9. It is quite simple, and the only decision you need to make is which grip is more suited to you.

Decide for yourself which one works for you by trying them all. You may find the Vardon grip suits you; it is certainly the most popular as people in general are stronger in the right hand than the left.

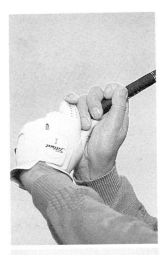

Figure 10 Hand position throughout the swing. Notice how the right hand rolls over the left hand after impact.

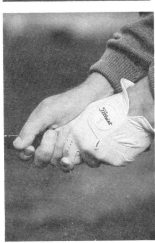

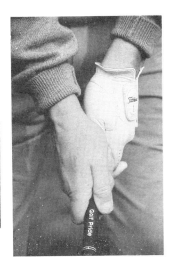

Impact position

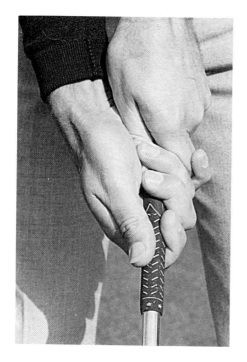

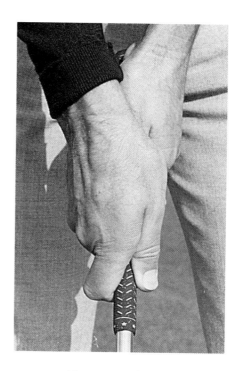

Figure 11 Strong grip.   Figure 12 Weak grip.

The interlocking grip may work best for you if you have short fingers and if it feels comfortable. Some golfers find it actually hurts to hold a club this way. But it does work, and very effectively. Jack Nicklaus has used it over the years, so no one can deny that it is well worth using.

If you have small hands (and this applies more to the ladies) try using the baseball grip. Don't be afraid to try it, it does give more power to the right hand and more feel of the club

Feel is something we should look for in the grip: don't just hold the club, hold it with feeling. This way you will be making the club part of you, and it will respond better to your instructions.

Last of all on the grip is the use of a glove. Is it really necessary? The answer is quite logical. If you do not use a glove then the club is more likely to twist in your hands, if contact with the ball is away from the centre of the club. Keeping the grips of your clubs tacky is another way to avoid this happening; one more reliability factor to consider for golf.

Reliability is one of the most fundamental of golf's keywords. Reliability of equipment, method, swing, and most definitely grip. For this we should use a glove. I know they seem a little expensive for what they are, but we buy them for what they do. They can be very much cheaper in the long run if we make them last longer by giving them a little more care. Usually, they are screwed up and stuffed into the bag, often with the balls, and left there until the next game. Take more care, don't roll them up. If this were the best way to keep them they would be sold like that. After a day when the glove, like you, has had a good soaking, why not drive home with it on, it will have a good chance then of drying to the right shape.

Having a good grip and constantly checking it out is our first priority. We can then get on with our next move - the stance.

FOUR

The Stance

A golf ball is tiny as balls go. It sits there on the ground or on a tee peg and our objective is to hit it from there to a place of our choice. It has a diameter of 1.68 inches and the world has a diameter of 14000 miles, and the idea is to hit the smaller one. It sounds quite simple, but I have seen even the most experienced of golfers miss them both. As you may know, it is called a fresh air shot and to avoid this very embarrassing situation, we must position ourselves correctly in relation to the ball. This is known as addressing the ball. There is a text book way of doing this and, no matter what standard of golfer you are, you should try to conform.

For the full shot, the feet at address should be as far apart as the width of your shoulders. If it is windy you may find it helps with your balance to widen your stance but shoulder width for all full shots is an accepted distance (figure 13).

When we swing the driver, the point of contact with the ground is somewhere near to a line drawn back to inside the left heel. This is why we position the ball there in order to hit the ball without first hitting the ground.

However, when playing iron shots this position does change. This is because of the reduced size of the swing arc, which makes the swing more of a down and through action, particularly for the shorter clubs. This again reduces the likelihood of grass getting between the ball and the club. If grass does get trapped then the friction between the club and the ball is reduced, resulting in loss of backspin. Backspin does improve however, if a little sand gets between the two by improving the frictional resistance. You must have noticed this when recovering from bunkers.

If you have the chance to tee up to play an iron shot, then do so. The ball will still be positioned in the same place within the stance and this is a much safer way to get the clean hit.

Backspin is achieved when the ball starts to leave the clubhead and of course varies according to the club used and the force applied (figure 14). The driver gives reduced amounts of backspin because of its face having little loft. The wedges, being of greater loft, sometimes produce too much backspin.

Because of the possibility of grass being caught between the ball and the clubface, I advise progressively moving the ball away from a line inside the left heel and nearer to

Figure 14 Ball impact.

21

Figure 13a The driver stance - the ball is positioned just inside the left heel.

Figure 13b Mid-iron stance - the ball is positioned mid-way between the feet.

Figure 13c Short-iron stance - the ball is positioned well back in the stance.

the right foot as the number on the iron gets larger. The shorter the iron gets, the nearer the ball gets to the right foot.

This moving of the ball along the line of the feet is not the only adjustment that must be made in order to obtain a perfect strike. We must be very careful how close we stand to the ball. When we play the driver we will automatically stand further away than when we play the wedge. But many golfers do not always get this distance correct. Very often we see large divots taken before the club makes contact with the ball and more often than not this is not a weight transfer problem; it is simply through playing the ball from too close to the feet.

You can find where to place the ball by standing at the address and holding a club as shown in figure 15. It is then lowered to the ground and the hands positioned below the line of your chin. Golfers who do this test, find their ball position slightly further away from their feet than they would normally play. It is far more important to have this correct than most golfers imagine.

Finding this place where the ball should be will ensure good balance and stop the reaching which results in either hitting the ball out of the heel of the club, or the cramped style which results in those dinner plate divots. I have actually seen these divots turn over and cover the ball.

If this distance is not calculated correctly you could find trouble from having the wrong lie of the club. You could make the club contact the ground heel first and turn the club to closed, alternatively toe contact will open the face with its obvious consequences.

Having decided the position of the hands at address your natural ability will decide which of the two recommended hand and arm alignment positions to adopt. The Y-stance is one as shown in figure 16 and the K-stance in figure 17. You will find that the Y-stance will hit the ball with a higher flight and the K-stance will keep the ball lower. Obviously I would advise the former if you have difficulty getting the ball in the air but a good reason for using the K-stance is that it has been used very successfully by Jack Nicklaus throughout his career.

Figure 18 shows the correct positioning with relation to the feet. What actually happens is that the shorter the irons get, and the further back they are, the nearer to the golfer they become. Even if the ball is positioned correctly we still have to remember the force generated in the downswing. Initially, this is not a large force, but as the swing gets into the hitting area, the force along the shaft increases to around 100 lbs. All of this downwards force is resisted by the legs and the back, and for this reason the legs and the back need to be strong. It is not surprising that we hear of golfers like Seve and Woosie having back problems. The further you hit the ball the larger the force.

In perspective, when a big hitting golfer strikes the ball he is resisting a force in his back which amounts to something like having a 1cwt hanging around his neck. This is why some golfers dip into the ball when trying to give the ball a little more muscle. Trying to knock the cover off the ball is not worth the effort, and it generally ends in failure. When

1

2

3

4

Figure 15 Finding where to place the ball.

Figure 16 Y-stance.

Figure 17 K-stance.

Figure 18 Ball and feet relationship.

trying to hit the ball, our main concern should be that of making good contact, well balanced and being well within the limits control. Of course this has to be in both the physical and mental sense.

AWKWARD LIES

The position in which we place our feet in relation to the ball position is quite easy to work out when we have a flat lie. It is not quite as easy if the ball sits higher or lower than our feet and other adjustments have to be made.

   The most important advice that I can give for playing from awkward lies is please swing within yourself. Do not try to knock the cover off the ball. Balancing from an uneven base is difficult enough without you generating swing forces that can throw you off balance. I would also recommend that you do not try to change the natural flight of the ball. The ball flight will curve according to the lie of the land. Trying to change this takes great skill and just like all other difficult shots we never practise them. So few golf club practise areas have facilities to practise shots from awkward lies. Maybe if club members requested such provisions then clubs might provide them. Knowing what the ball will do when we play from an awkward lie has to be known. Doubt and uncertainty always reduce our chance of success.

   The changes to the stance are quite obvious but still need to be explained. If the slope of the land leaves you standing with your left foot higher than your right (figure 19) then you will have to position the ball further forward. This change of position means that a clean hit will impart an anticlockwise spin into the ball, hence its tendency to hook or draw. It happens because the club face will have closed by the time it reaches the ball. This type of lie also encourages the golfer to hit behind the ball, because the body weight may stay on the back foot. It can be a little difficult to get correct weight transfer and even if we do manage to get our weight forward and hit the ball clean, it will climb too high. When faced with this shot we should remember that the trajectory of the ball will be higher and allow for this by taking more club. This is another shot to practise so that you know your distances.

   There is the other case where the ball must be moved backwards towards the right foot (figure 20). This changes the swing plane (in the other direction) and the ball will slice or fade during flight. Again balance can be affected and the awful topped shot can be the result. This type of lie sends the ball off on a lower trajectory, therefore less club will be required to cover a normal distance.

   When the land slopes the other way (figures 21a + 21b) the ball can be either above or below the feet. In this case, the position of the ball in relation to the left heel along the line to the target, does not change from that of the flat lie. What does change however, is its distance from the front of you. If the ball has to be a little nearer to you then shorten your grip on the club for the uphill lie, and lengthen it in the other case.

Figure 19

Figure 20

Figure 21a

Figure 21b

Uphill, downhill and hillside stances.

Of course we have not finished yet. What if there are combinations of these slopes? There invariably are, as we all know, and there is one simple way to make sure you have the ball positioned in the correct place. If you find yourself in such a situation take notice when you take your practise swing just where you make contact with the ground. The ball will then be positioned just behind this in relation to your feet. I suppose you could use this method for all of the shots you play, but not of course for shots from hazards. As you know, a club must not be grounded before you play from a hazard, and just to remind you, if the ball does not come out at the first attempt from sand, do not repair the sand until it is out.

FIVE

The Swing

The way we stand to address the ball will determine just how good a contact we make between the club and the ball. The next thing we have to get correct is how to deliver maximum club head velocity in the hitting area of the swing. What we are asking for is to hit the ball with "good timing".

All of the important body movements needed to complete a good swing have to be listed. This is important for the beginner and for swing fault finding. For the beginner it's just like learning to drive. You have to keep looking where the pedals are for a while until you find them automatically.

Even when you have developed a good swing routine, changes can occur. This happens to all golfers and we have to be able to identify the parts of our swing if we develop a fault. Faults can be rhythm and timing faults, or changes in our swing plane. There are many other possible corrections which we may have to make, so we must be able to separate the different parts of our swing. We cannot go and ask the pro in the middle of a competition round just what is going wrong, but we should consult him as soon as we can.

When we start to play golf we can fall into the trap of trying to follow all of the listed body movements and this is impossible. We are asked to take the club back and move the left knee inwards until it points at the ball. Well it's more difficult to stop this happening than it is consciously trying to do it. Many of your body movements are fully automatic and you should consciously consider only two or three. Three is perhaps maximum in the time you have available. One to start, one on the way back and one to start down.

The swing should start from a good stance with a good grip. With the left arm straight but not rigid and the club is taken back along a line from the target to the ball. Of course this is only a guide line to start the club back. The turning of the shoulders brings the club head inside the line. Don't try to keep the club head close to the ground - this will only encourage you to tilt your shoulders which is another successful way of taking dinner plate divots.

The shoulder turn is a pivoting action and some golfers can achieve a good shoulder turn without raising their left heel from the ground. Obviously all golfers cannot do this and some teachers do ask for the left heel to clear the ground on the way back. If it does remain on the ground the foot will tilt slightly through the movement of the knee and again it is difficult not to do this.

The club will carry on until it reaches a position at the top where it is parallel to the ground and pointing at the target. The right elbow will be tucked in to the right side and the left arm will be straight. Well that's what the classical swing teacher will tell you.

Some of us cannot reach this position and the top of our swing is where we can comfortably finish. It's no good trying to reach a position not suitable for your physical make up and then loose control at the top. You have to be in a position to start a controlled downswing and not be too tense. There are differing arguments as to how much tension you should have in your body at the top of your backswing and I would suggest - as little as you can manage. You have to be correctly balanced at this time in your swing and too much muscular tension may put you off balance and, more importantly, make you start your downswing too quickly.

The wrist action in this first half of the swing will be automatically decided by the weight of the club.

Beginners may find the position at the top of the swing quite difficult to hold and can only reach the top when the club is in motion. Well this is normal and until the swing has been practised for a while it may be difficult. Don't worry, you will get there.

The right leg action in the first part of the swing should be firmly fixed to its start position. The legs should be slightly bent throughout the swing, firstly to give fluidity of movement, and secondly to cushion the downwards force we talked about earlier. Incidentally, I am very fortunate that the firm knee requirement is in the right knee and not the left. The luck we get in life and golf is not always bad. Sometimes the kicks are to our advantage and there are times when we should regard ourselves as being very fortunate.

On the downswing the wrists stay cocked, until they are about waist height from the ground. They then start to uncock - again automatically due to the force produced by the clubhead and assisted by the hitting force of the hands and arms. This action increases the speed of the clubhead to maximum speed at impact. If this uncocking of the wrists is activated too early maximum speed will also come too early. In many cases an early hitting method means that the club head will be reducing speed in the hitting area and results in a loss of distance.

This early action which is used by a large proportion of golfers is activated by the golfer trying to hit the ball too hard. Better results will be achieved by relying more on speed and less on effort. Hit too early and you will never get your weight transfer correct. Being left with your weight on the right foot at the time of impact, is a good method for hitting bad shots. The correct action is achieved by regarding the downswing as a "Pulling the Bell Rope" action.

You will notice that the position of the body at impact is not the same as at the address position. It has to change to compensate for the forwards force of the swing, otherwise you would fall over or more likely walk after the ball (figure 22).

Looking at the legs in the downswing we see that through the twisting motion of the hips they have changed to a braced left leg and the right leg is starting to follow the action of the swing.

Figure 22 The braced left side is to
assist balance at impact.

At the point of impact it is also very noticeable that both arms are reasonably straight to withstand the large force acting down and through the shaft. The shoulders are square to the intended line and the heel of the right foot is starting to leave the ground.

This again is a position achieved by the more competent golfer and many golfers find that to have their shoulders slightly open at impact will help to square up the club face. Many ladies use this swing action to great effect.

The follow through turns the head, shoulders and hips to face the target and if you can attain this position you have a much better chance of playing a good shot.

Many golfers have very little follow through and cut off this very important part of the swing because of their anxiety to follow the ball. Finishing the swing too early also evolves from hitting too early. I think it would be very safe to say that when Seve starts to manage without a follow through, then you can.

These movements of the swing are automatic to some extent, but only to those who are "natural" ball players. That is to say, those who find the game reasonably easy to play right from the start. Many of these "naturals" become professionals or very good amateurs but there are many others who do not find the game quite so easy.

There are those who find the body movements difficult to coordinate and for these we should list the body movements. It will then be a matter for them to check if their movements are in the correct order and if they are not, making sure that they are. The following 15 points should be checked.

Figure 23a Stance.

1. Using any club, take your stance square to your intended swing line with your feet as far apart as your shoulder width.

2. Your left foot may be square to the line or just open, the right foot must be square to the line.

3. Whichever method of grip you use, the back of your left hand must be in line with the club face and be facing the target.

4. Your weight should be evenly distributed on each leg giving a good feeling of balance. At no time must you lean on the club when in the address position.

Figure 23b Close-up of feet and club position.

5.   The club itself is rested gently on the ground, with the arms being quite straight and the hands positioned vertically below the chin.

Figure 24a The takeaway.

6.   The takeaway must be in one piece and involves the hands, the arms and the shoulders moving together. This creates a twisting motion from the waist and a slight shift of weight to the right side.

7.   Just after the arms begin to move backwards the wrists start their "cocking" action and the full cocking action is reached at the top of the swing.

Figure 24b The takeaway.

8. The club is now parallel to the ground and pointing at the target. The left leg is slightly bent and its knee points towards the ball, with the shoulders fully turned and square to the line.

9. The grip at this point can become quite loose. Make sure this does not happen. Maintain a firm but not tight grip so as not to create too much tension in your hands and arms.

Figure 25 Pulling the bell rope.

10. From the top the club is pulled down to waist height without any uncocking of the wrists. The hips will start to open as the weight transfer takes place from the right to the left side of the body.

11. With the club at waist height the face is still open and it is here where it starts to return to square as the right arm straightens and the hands return to the address position.

Figure 26 The point of impact.

12.   At the point of impact, both arms are reasonably straight and the forwards
      action of the hit puts more weight onto the left side. The heel of the right
      foot will be lifting off the ground and the right knee will be bent and
      pointing towards the ball.

Figure 27 Just after impact.

13. Just after impact the shoulders will start to open quite quickly with the lifting of the head and the right arm taking on a straight line position in line with the target.

Figure 28 The follow-through.

14. The classic finish of the follow-through sees the major part of the torso facing the target. The right foot will be on its toe, the left foot on its outer side and the hands high above the left shoulder.

15. The most significant part of the finish position is its balanced and statue like pose.

Swing faults

Assuming we have gripped the club correctly and used the correct address procedure, there are certain common swing faults which we should try to avoid. Some of them are similar by being incomplete parts of the swing.

a.   The backswing for instance, does not always get completed and results in poor "tempo". (The backswing being your backswing). If it is too short there is less time to return the club face back to square and shots are lost to the right. Short backswing golfers have to remember to use less physical effort and to replace this with better rhythm.

b.   The wrists are sometimes wrongly rolled open on the backswing and then left open during the downswing. This is caused either by not knowing the wrists have to return to the address position or tension in the wrists when trying to give the ball a little extra force. An over tight grip will restrict movement of the wrists and fore arms making it impossible to roll the club face back to square.

c.   The follow-through is neglected mainly for reasons which I have already mentioned. I must emphasise again - if you have no follow-through your weight will be on the wrong foot and, almost certainly, the ball will go anywhere but straight and you may hit the ball "fat".

Other faults do occur. The swing plane can be either too flat or too upright, which is bound to create problems (figure 29). Here again stature is the dominant feature, a small person will have a flat swing and a tall person an upright one. One way to decide where your hands should be at the top is to draw an imaginary line from your hands at address through your right shoulder. Your hands at the top must be on this line.

Hooking and Slicing

Hooking and slicing can be two major assets to the golfer. Unfortunately, they happen when they are not wanted and are the most common of faults. The main cause of these is bad technique, and they are not only brought about by purely physical means, they are often brought about by mental stress. Any situation which induces stress, be it anger, fear, anxiety, or excitement, will promote changes from our normal swing movements.

The most common way golfers slice or hook when they do not want to, happens when they are trying to give the ball that little bit extra. This encourages the slicer to stay on their back foot or in the case of those who have a tendency to hook then the right hand comes over the top at impact and the hook is played.

Figure 29a Flat swing.

Figure 29b Upright swing.

Figure 29c Correct swing.

During any round of golf there is always a time when we purposely need to hook or slice. Some holes are designed this way, so we must learn how to produce the curving shot when it is needed. If we understand how to play the shot when we need it, then correcting it when it "creeps" into your game will be much easier.

The slice or fade is produced basically by having the shoulders and the feet aligned left of the target. If, together with this, we return the club face back square to the line at impact, we will produce the fade and, if it is open at impact, the slice.

To do this, the set procedure would be to first position the ball forward of its normal position within the stance. Address the ball with an open stance and a square or slightly open club face. The club would then be taken back along a line outside of the target line which would encourage the right elbow to "fly" (figure 30). Through doing this the right fore arm which would normally be in the vertical plane at the top of the backswing, would be more towards the horizontal. From the top of the swing the downward movement should start with an opening of the shoulders instead of waiting for this to happen naturally at the time of impact with the ball. After impact there is a tendency to lean away from the ball position and not the normal upright finish to the swing.

Figure 30 Flying right elbow. We know this can work as Eamon Darcy has proved. But it is not recommended.

To hook we would do much of the opposite. The ball position would be further back in the stance and the feet and shoulders in a line to the right of the target. To draw the ball we would need to swing along an in to out line and return the face back to square. If more movement is needed and we need to hook the ball, then at impact the face would have to be slightly closed.

At the top of the backswing the right elbow would need to be quite tightly into the right side.

In the downswing the hands and the club must move from inside to outside the line by restricting the hip action. The hips should be kept as square to the line as is possible and not be allowed the natural opening action of the normal swing.

High or Low Shots

Quite often during a round we find we are faced with a shot which demands that we play the ball with a high or low trajectory.

A rainy day on the 11th at St Andrews.

On many of the links courses, particularly in Scotland, the weather can be the main hazard. In any game we may play, we often find awkward places where we have to go over or under trees. Whatever the reasons we must know how to play the shot.

When it is required, the low shot should be played with a straight faced club. It has a low take off trajectory and low spin. This is a delicate shot and requires more than the normal number of practise swings to get the feel of it. Even then it is so easy to snatch at the shot and hit behind the ball. Put this in your practise schedule where there is no pressure to bear, and get to know the "feeling". It is one of those very useful shots which come around quite often, so we must know how to play it. A loose grip is essential for playing this shot.

In the case of the high shot the club face can be opened slightly. A ball hit this way will fly higher than normal and have a slight fade, so allow for this happening. This is the only shot in golf where you can justify a tighter grip on the club to make extra sure that the club face stays open.

Advice on how to swing and stand to play a golf shot cannot vary a lot. To a large extent it is common sense, and those who are prepared to look at golf through logical eyes stand a better chance at being good at the game.

The difficulties some people have are often self-inflicted by trying to cure a fault with a fault. In the end, common sense must tell them that if they continue to practise this way they will never achieve their ambitions. There are no gimmicks that work in golf. Try to look good when swinging a club and you have a better chance of producing good results.

SIX

The Short Game

There is a shot in golf which some golfers find easy to play and others find very difficult. This is the shot which is less than 100yds long and requires only part of a full swing. It is a "feel" shot; difficult enough when there is no pressure, but when there is, it demands nerves of steel.

How can I get the distance? How can I find the line? What type of shot should I play? Should I pitch it up to the flag or run it up? These are the sort of questions which churn around in the mind. Decisions, decisions, decisions; culminating in so much doubt it is no wonder many golfers find the shot difficult.

The main reason for making a mess of the shot lies in the mental rehearsal process; we do not use a positive picture. We stand over the shot and can't decide how to play it. There are so many nerve racking thoughts which make it difficult to play any particular shot. How on earth can we play a shot if we cannot first decide which type of shot to play? All of this over a period of time which stretches out far longer than for normal shots. It is this type of golf stress which we must learn to avoid. If we don't then tiredness will invade our golf long before the end of a game.

I know there is perhaps more to consider around the greens; slope, speed, etc., but far too much time is spent thinking about these shots. When the pressure is on, why do we take such a long time to play the shot? The "swing sequence" must be the same for every shot - he who hesitates is lost.

It would seem that some golfers, professionals included, do not understand how to mentally deal with short shots. To be positive with their effort, they must learn to take the least amount of time possible to play the shot. I don't mean rush, just don't dilly dally about: make up your mind which shot to play and then play it. It's the hanging about making unnecessary enquiry which in the end results in confusion and the sometimes pathetic attempt to play what should be a simple shot.

Being such a simple shot makes the embarrassment of fluffing it so unbearable. It is the same with the short putt, we make them difficult in our belief that there is no excuse if we miss.

Much of our swing movements in golf are decided automatically. We organise these movements by the way we practise. Our ability to judge distance is also mainly automatic.

If we hit the ball clean on say a 50 yard pitch, we get the distance reasonably correct nearly every time. So to accept that the human mind can deal with this is the first thing we must do. The second consideration we have to make, is what to do about line and this is not a difficult process either.

We mostly hit shots off line through our anxious mind believing that we will possibly get it wrong. We come off the ball before the shot is complete and go left, or we "steer" it and hit the ball right. All of the time we have been considering getting it wrong, so how can we get it right? You should accept that your automatic self will do exactly as you ask it. If you tell it to get it wrong, it will oblige. It will also fail with regard to line or length if you do not offer any line or length to your instruction. Golfers these days seem so taken up by "how" to play a particular shot that they forget the instruction of "what" shot they are about to play.

The procedure to play any shot has to follow a complete thought routine. We should first decide on the type of shot we have to play, and make sure it is the correct one. Next, we must practise the swing we need and then without delay stand to the ball and play the shot. Keep it simple and it is simple, make it complicated and you will never get it right. Just watch the American stars and copy their method - they get on with it.

Pitching

This is the name we give to the shot which carries all the way to the place we want it to stop. If the ground is very wet we can pitch to the inch. It is sometimes necessary to pitch it short if we are unable to generate much backspin or the greens are hard and if we are pitching onto a down slope.

There are two ways to reduce the force of the full shot and there is one which I would recommend more than the other. One is to use less wrist action and use just the arms to generate club head speed and the other way is to reduce the force of a hit by reducing the length of the swing. Players who do have the ability to play this more wristy shot are usually very good short game players. But I would suggest that the more reliable way is to use the firm wrist method and swing across the line. It is similar to the sand bunker shot and very good at getting out of all kinds of trouble.

On many of our more famous golf courses in the UK the fairways are fringed with heather. They are very nice places to play golf and the heather is nice until you have to play from it. You cannot always get a club to the back of the ball and the only way to hit it is to come across the line. Even if you have to come across the line so far that you almost hit your left foot with the club, firm up on the wrist action and the ball will still come out clean.

Chipping

The other way to get up and down in two, as we call it, is to be able to chip well. This is a shot we play with a straight faced club, although some golfers prefer to use a wedge and have their hands well forwards of the club head. This gives the same loft as using a straight faced club and gives the same ball position for every shot. Adjustments have to be made only for angle of loft.

The line of swing is normally along the intended line and this is the way most golfers play the shot. It is just a case of setting the ball on its way, using your judgement and the contours of the land to determine where the ball finishes. This is a real feel shot and unlike the pitch, when we can assume the ground to be flat for all shots, we need to be able to read the greens.

The "run up", as the shot is often called, is more used by amateurs than professionals; it is, or seems to be, more easy to play. I suppose it is used when we do not have to go over obstacles, so the fear aspect of the pitch is slightly reduced. It is also played with a more upright swing, and this also helps remove the possibility of hitting behind the ball (figure 31).

Figure 31 Stance to play the run up shot.

These short shots are not the ones I see amateurs practise. It is just as important to keep reminding yourself how to play this shot as it is any other shot. In fact it is perhaps more important to the amateur, who misses more greens than the pro, to be confident of getting up and down in two. The professionals practise them daily particularly during tournaments. They will always hit 25 or so before leaving the practise area for the putting green (figure 32).

Figure 32 Practising short shots.

One shot the amateur does play more than the pro is the "Texas Wedge" (figure 33). For those who do not understand, this means taking the putter before you get to the green. The shot asks for a lot of confidence in judging the distance but at the same time, not many golfers take too much divot with a putter, and it is almost impossible to shank - or is it?

Figure 33 The Texas Wedge.

It would be of help for all amateurs to know just how the ball will run after it is chipped with any one of the clubs in the bag. For instance do you know how far a 3 iron will run on after it is chipped 6 feet through the air, compared with the same distance chipped with a 9 iron? You should: it is no good thinking you know, get to know.

The Stance to Pitch and Chip

Once we have decided to play one particular shot, we have to take out stance. For both the pitch and the chip, the stance is the same (Figure 34). The feet should be quite close together and be no more than 12 inches apart. The ball position within the feet can be as far back as the right foot, although normally one would play the shot from somewhere near centre (figure 35).

For all short shots around the greens the swing does not reach more than waist height on both the backswing and the follow-through. The follow-through is perhaps the main feature of these little shots. If you do quit at the point of impact then all sorts of nasties can happen.

Pitching and chipping are departments of the game for saving shots. They provide a wonderful feeling when we get them right, but get them wrong and the feelings are not very nice at all.

Figure 34 Stance for chipping. Weight forward on the left foot.

Figure 35 Stance for pitching. Weight more evenly distributed on both feet.

SEVEN

Sand Bunkers

Sand bunkers are built into golf courses for one reason alone; to make the golfer think. They are not there to instill the anger and fear for which they are more renowned. They are there to make the game more interesting it would be a very boring game if we played in a flat field with no obstacles.

Sand bunkers are positioned to send the golfer along a predetermined route to the green. It is not the intention of the designer to make you go into a bunker but he does expect you think about how to keep out of one. Yes, fear does come into the reckoning and the best way to overcome this is to know not only how to get out of them but how to keep out of them.

If there is a bunker down the right side of the fairway at a distance of 220 yds from the tee, and this is where your drive would normally finish, then play short. If you do take your driver and find the sand, don't feel angry, feel stupid. Of course many of the times we do visit sand it is not because of bad judgement of distance, it is because we play a bad shot. Whether this is caused by a technical fault or one of the many emotional hazards we find at golf is another thing.

I cannot help repeating that golf is a game of common sense. Certainly the more skilful you are, the less you will visit the sand, but common sense is your best "shot".

Being confident in playing the bunker shot is just as important as it is with any other shot. Gary Player is confident and you don't need me to tell you why (figure 36). Motivation can be the most difficult problem, but if the facilities are not provided by your club, then practise is rather difficult. If only all golf clubs had adequate bunker practise facilities I am sure golfers would make good use of them. Surely one more bunker to maintain is not too much of a hardship for the green staff.

When playing from sand, many golfers find they take too much sand. By this I mean they hit too far behind the ball and "dig deep". This often ends with the ball staying in the bunker and it has the chance of rolling back into the same hole. If it does, it then becomes a more difficult shot, so first time out is our main objective.

Hitting behind the ball whether it is in the bunker or on the fairway, is mainly related to poor weight distribution. Standing to take the shot with an open stance and constantly looking up, does encourage too much weight to be on the back foot. So make a conscious check of your weight distribution and make sure that it is evenly distributed on both feet. Having said that, if you do have to guard against flying over the green then weight on the back foot will solve the problem. It will also reduce the fear and give you the confidence to play the shot.

Figure 36 Gary Player from the sand.

One other thing about taking too much sand. When you stand to play a bunker shot, you don't shuffle about simply because everybody else does: you do it to get the firmest foot hold possible. Get down to firm ground, because if you don't you will be sliding about on loose sand. Balance can only be achieved from a sound base. You must also remember that bunker play requires that you make one very important adjustment to your grip. The depth of the sand, when you have shuffled down into it, leaves you with the ball above the level of your feet. When the ball is well above your feet you must grip lower down the shaft by the same amount as the depth of the sand. If the sand is two inches deep then go two inches down the shaft.

Fairway bunkers and those awkward ones about 50yds or so from the green very much need this method of grip and stance preparation. The stance you use for taking full shots is very much the first priority when considering which shot to play. If when playing this shot your stance is not stable and firm then don't look for miracles and go for the "big one".

A typical long shot example of playing from the fairway bunkers is the 18th at The Belfry. If there is any possibility of coming up short with the shot, then lay up, just ask Ray Floyd (figure 37). He was forced into having a go in the final round of the 1986 Ryder Cup and if an experienced player like Ray fails, there is not much chance of a less talented player getting it right.

Figure 37 Raymond Floyd.

This again raises the question, "How far can you play this long bunker shot - with any club in the bag?" Knowing your distances is one of the basic requirements for golf.

The short bunker shots around the greens are often referred to as "feel" shots. The stance should be as figure 38 with the ball just in front of centre and the swing will be across the line - out to in - according to distance required. If you have an ordinary lie then the club face should be slightly open. With the "fried egg" type of lie (figure 39) then better results are obtained by closing the face of the club to allow for the sand to open the club face.

Figure 38 Short bunker stance.

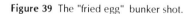

Figure 39 The "fried egg" bunker shot.

There is another bunker problem which leaves many golfers wanting and this is what to do if the sand is wet. Under normal rain conditions this just means being careful but if the sand is exceptionally wet, use the wedge and not the sand iron. Your wedge will dig into the sand as it would take a divot on the fairway. The design of your sand iron will encourage it to bounce off the wet sand.

Most bunkers allow the chance of making up for a bad shot, if you can get up and down in two, you could even hole the shot. Lee Trevino seems to be very good at this. Some may say he is very lucky, I would say it is more likely to be his practise paying off.

As I have said before, the best way to deal with bunkers is to keep out of them in the first place and this goes for that other difficult hazard - water.

Other Trouble

The unfortunate thing about playing over water is that if you go in, the shot has gone and cannot be retrieved - just like the ball on most occasions. I think that golf course designers can overdo including the water hazard, and The Belfry is a typical example. It introduces too much fear into a game which is supposed to be such a pleasure to play.

I see no reason for putting the golfer in a position where fear, anger and the resulting depression are too much a part of the game. Instead of making the game more interesting it can force players away, one game may be enough for some less talented players. Courage has always been part of our game, but there is a limit to this, and pleasure has to come first.

Relief from an unplayable lie varies considerably. The drop from a water hazard is different from that of a lateral water hazard, and so on. There are drops and drops - find out which is which or you may find "disqualified" by the side of your name on the winners list. I know some golfers who find the rules boring to study and rely on asking others, but the rules are there for your pleasure, so read them. It saves lots of time and arguing if you are up to date.

Having to take a drop is not always necessary. If possible you can play the shot as it lies. In the 1985 US Masters Curtis Strange had the choice at the 13th. It was debatable whether or not to play the shot and he opted to have a go. In the end it proved to be the wrong thing to do, he muffed the shot and lost the Masters.

He lost not because he should have taken a drop, but because of the total situation surrounding the shot. Was it because he should have laid up short of the water? I think it was. He was so pumped up at the time and his confidence was running high. He would have been better to think of mentally staying "up" and not risking going "down". The state of shock as the commentator so rightly put it, reduced him to a mere mortal. I don't think he will do the same again if he has the chance, he is far too intelligent a player.

Difficult Lies

There are less punishing places we can find ourselves in at golf, and where there is no need to take a drop. Places which can still force the red face to appear - if you let them. The old divot hole is one and is a constant problem to me. If you find yourself in one, get on and do the best you can, and don't complain if you do not know how to deal with the shot. What club should I use to play the shot? How will the ball react? Will it come out high or low? How far will it travel? Find out on the practise ground.

We find places on some fairways at all courses where dips in the fairway gather the ball into a small area. Needless to say these areas are divot hole traps. It is normally a short distance from a green, hence the large divot holes. We can usually make the green by using one more club, but do be careful not to push the ball right. Try not to give the shot that little extra, and have faith in your club selection. If you want to play a punched shot use a little more club and allow for reduced backspin.

Another situation to make you think is when you have a tree or some other obstacle in the way of your swing. This is a real club-bending possibility, especially if you allow anger to help you to play the shot. Be patient and play the ball out, after all you hit it there. If you happen to be playing foursomes, then don't moan at your partner if he did it. He would not have done it on purpose and will be depressed enough without you knocking him further down.

Sometimes, the lie you find asks you to try your luck at playing the opposite handed shot. You do not have to be quite so lucky with the outcome if you know how to play it. You must try to play the other hand because it is asked for quite often. The putter is the tool most easily used for this job, but if it does not have a flat back then the back of a straight faced club will trundle the ball along. I personally have only one shot to play in these situations: maybe you should do the same. It means I only have to practise this one shot and it is the only one to use if you have a bad lie, or need a little loft (figure 40).

The shot which seems to trouble the amateur more than it should is the one from semi rough. He always seems to take too much club. What he should first decide is not which club will cover the distance, but which club will hit the ball clean.

To the professional the semi rough shot is less of a problem and we have to ask why this is, and take note. As I said earlier, he makes full use of club head speed as opposed to muscle power. He knows that grass is an easy material to cut, even with the bluntest of instruments and does not look upon it as a restriction to the swing. The only thing he needs to consider is the reduced grip between the club and the ball which is significant for backspin. Any grass which gets in between the two reduces the spin rate.

Figure 40 From my experience this is the most reliable way to play the left-handed shot .

Most golfers do not take enough care when selecting a club for a bad lie. Club selection depends on the lie, the steepness of the swing and the flier. Long irons do tend to mean failure for the amateur so only use them if the lie is a good one. If you have no alternative because of over hanging trees, then slow the swing down and don't dig too deep.

If you are unsure of hitting the ball any distance from a semi rough lie, then don't use an iron club, use a wood. The four or five wood is a very good tool for this job. It will part the grass instead of cutting it. This happens because the club has a cupped bottom and presses the grass sideways as it comes into the ball. The only thing you have to watch is that the ball does not pop up and the club go right underneath it, as it may do when sitting in spongy grass.

I know I keep harping on about how far you can hit the ball with different clubs and from different lies, but I hope you are seeing the logic behind it. When you practise, play some shots from the edge of the semi and some from the semi, you will then be able to measure the difference quite easily (figure 41).

The deep rough is a very different proposition, and usually leaves no option but to just get out. Don't try to gain too much distance if it will only change your next shot from say a six iron to a seven. Be sensible and take the easy way out. Don't allow the possibility of staying in, it will only add to the mental strain and make things worse. Playing the easy way out is not just for physical reasons, its main objective is to reduce mental stress.

Trouble shots are the ones which eat away at your reserves of mental energy. You can guard against them to some extent by taking every game as an adventure. Very rarely does even the elite pro get through a round without some form of trouble shot. Enjoy the challenge and the intrigue of your golf. You would perhaps be playing some other game if golf were too easy.

Figure 41 Playing from the semi rough.
Position the ball back in the stance.

EIGHT

Putting

When you win the putts have dropped. It is a must on the professional tour, if you don't putt well you don't make money. In the 1986 Swiss Open I putted reasonably well for a level par score after two rounds and failed to make the cut. Three under par was needed to qualify so I was on the early plane home. It was once said "you drive for show and you putt for dough" and how true this is.

Over the years I have seen great men crumble over short putts. There have always been the "yippers", those who lose control on the greens. They freeze and have great difficulty taking the putter back. Their shattered minds just cannot cope. Some top professionals have had to give up the game, whereas others have fought and overcome the problem.

Putting is the other half of the game; reasonably easy in practise, but knee-trembling in competition. Actually it's not just the knees which wobble, it's everything. When the pressure is on, distance is a strain to get right and the lining up of those short ones is terrifying.

Putting is mostly in the mind and it's here where it can all start to go wrong. This is one department of the complete golfer which we must all understand. We cannot be anything like proficient as a golfer if we do not know what to do mentally, as well as physically, about putting . Dennis Vardy explains the mental game in his book* and you should all read it.

Physically it does not appear to be too difficult. There are so many stances, grips and swings which all seem to work. They all sink those three footers and so method does not seem to matter too much.

My observations tell me differently. All of the great putters, Bob Charles and Tom Kite, to name just two, use a very straight forward method. They use none of the gimmicks, funny grips and odd stances we see when we are out playing.

Then again, some of these odd looking methods do work. They have to or their owners would have abandoned them long ago. We see short grips, long grips, overlapping grips, split hand grips, side winder grips and the reverse hand grip (figure 42) and of course the Bernhard Langer anti-yip grip which is extremely effective.

These are just a few of the more straight forward grips, there are others so complicated I couldn't describe them. And why do people do it? Is it because they are looking for some secret method or is it because they don't really know what they are doing? A bit of both I would say.

* "The Mental Game of Golf" published by Castle Publications

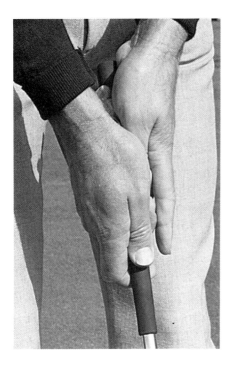
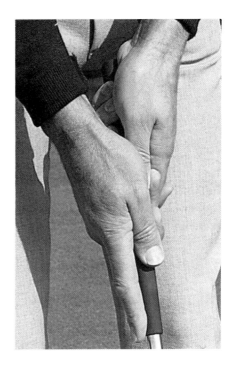

Figure 42 Various putting grips.

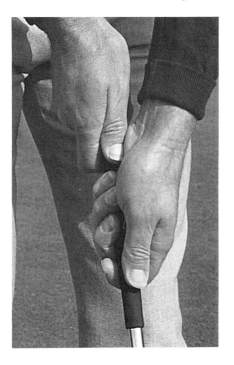
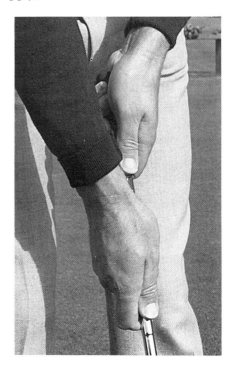

The way some of them stand for a start is sometimes quite funny. Some are too upright, some are crouched over so much that they appear to be looking through their legs. I once saw one lady actually standing with her back to the hole.

All of this must seem very misleading and confusing to the beginner and the beginning is where we must all start to examine putting. We have to know exactly what to do and how to do it. The object is to hit a ball with a putter across a green and into the hole.

First of all we must stand correctly. We must position ourselves in such a way, that when we swing the putter and hit the ball, it will travel in the direction we want it to.

Good lining up is one of the difficulties of putting. Even if we get this right, the speed at which the ball travels is also of great importance. It has been calculated that the speed of the ball when it reaches the hole must be within the range of zero to 4.7 ft/sec. If it is not within this range then it will either be short or jump over the hole. It will jump over because less than half of the ball will be below ground. If it is travelling at the maximum speed, the line of the ball must be on the centre of the hole. If it is not the ball will not have the time for gravity to act upon it, and will lip out.

The beginner may quickly come to the conclusion that the best way to line up is to stand in the same way as if he were playing croquet, with one foot either side of the line. This is a very good method as was proved by Sam Snead. Unfortunately, it was decided that this method contravened the rules. It was made illegal because the rules say, "The game of golf is basically a game of skill". It was felt that if the golfer wished to stand facing the hole he must stand with both feet to one side of the line.

There are many ways to stand to putt, but only two swing methods. One is a push action and the other a hit action. The choice is made by trying both methods and using the one which works the best.

Method one, the push action, can be used with any type of stance, from the sidewinder to standing parallel to the line. The swing is performed with no cocking of the wrists and the line of the swing is as near as possible to the line of the putt. Reducing wrist action is quite commonly used and can be done by firming up your grip. If you watch Tom Watson (figure 43) you will see that his knuckles are white when he putts. Tom has always been a very good putter and his method is copied by many golfers. But if you are a little on the nervous side when you putt then beware, holding the club too tightly will create muscular tension and this you must avoid.

I have used the push action for many years with some success. I stand square to the line and have my putter shaft adjusted to position my hands behind the position of the ball. I swing along the line, my wrists are quite firm, and the ball is pushed along to the hole without a definite hit at the ball.

Method two is the hit action and is more like a small swing. The blade of the putter opens in the back swing and returns to square at the impact position. After the ball has been hit with a definite hitting action the putter face then closes on the follow through.

Figure 43 Tom Watson.

Both methods work fine. The only criticism for the first method is that when the "pressure" is on, it can happen that the blade may be left open at the contact position with the ball.

Choosing your putter

Putters come in all sorts of weights and shapes. We are always reading that this putter is better than that, and it is for you to decide. Your basic requirement is to determine whether you must push or hit to find a consistent stroke.

If you are a push putter, then you would be wise to use a face balanced putter (figures 44 + 45). I have used one for most of my career and therefore find other balanced putters tend to "wobble" on the back swing. Those of you who get better results using a hitting action would be better advised to use a heel shafted putter, in other words a "blade" type. They act very similarly to the rest of your clubs, and help you to repeat your swing action.

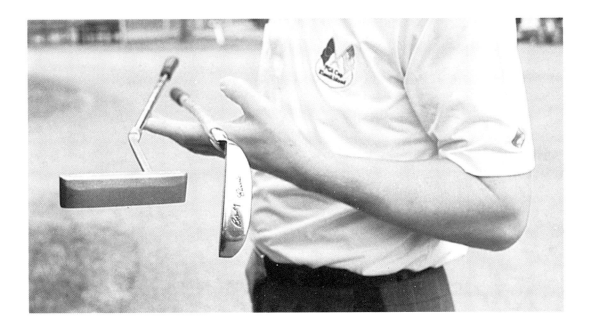

Figure 44 The face balanced putter is on the left.

Figure 45 Various putters.

When you hit a ball with a putter you will use a variation of hits just like in the rest of your game. By this I mean you will sometimes top it, hit it on its centre, below its centre, on the upswing or on the down swing. You will also sometimes, slice it, hook it, push it and pull it. Obviously you will not get the same amount of movement because the ball is in contact with the ground, but you will get some reaction from the ball.

If we look at these actions one by one we will then be able to determine which is more reliable, we will also be able to see which ones we must do our utmost to avoid.

1. Hitting the ball on its centre (figure 46)

If you hit a ball in this way it will skid for the first few inches of its travel. On very fast greens this may be an advantage but the ball will read any imperfections in the surface and bounce up or kick left or right.

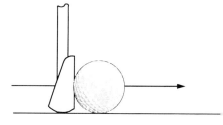

Figure 46

2. Hitting on the upswing. (figure 47)

This is a feature of the swing of all good putters, and will give the ball an overspin. This overspin will help the ball ride over any imperfections in the first part of its travel and because of this will run more true to its intended line. It may start off with a little jump but in this case it is not a bounce and not detrimental to distance.

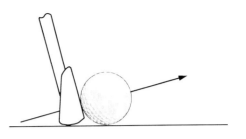

Figure 47

3. Hitting the ball on the downswing. (figure 48)

This is a method which creates errors and is not to be recommended. Any ball given a hit which involves any downwards force, will induce a backspin of some degree. You should avoid this happening because it will also increase any left or right swing if you inadvertently hit the ball with an open or closed face. Under normal circumstances any ball hit downwards will have a tendency to bounce and this will reduce its forwards motion.

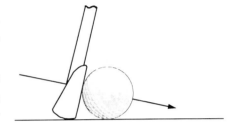

Figure 48

4. The fade and the draw. (figure 49)

This is a problem we all face from time to time and is due to having the ball positioned wrongly within our stance. Wrong position will encourage you to swing the club across the line, so if this is a problem of yours then try to keep the putter swing more square to the line. Of all the faults which creep in to everyone's game this is perhaps the most common and the easiest to cure.

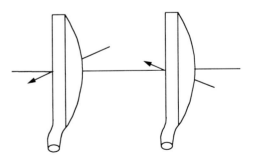

Figure 49

5. The slice or the hook. (figure 50)

It may seem unlikely to you that this might happen, but from my research I have been able to conclude that it does happen. As a matter of fact most golfers do one or the other. It is far easier to swing in to out or surprisingly out to in than it is to swing the club straight. Even if the push method is used, the path of the club is an arc and not a straight line.

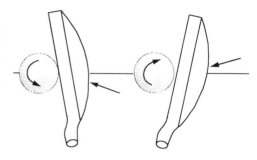

Figure 50

6. The push with an open faced putter. (figure 51)

This is the worst fault of all and the reason why we miss those short ones. "How on earth could I miss from such a short distance?" we often ask ourselves. "I didn't even hit the hole." Well there has to be some reason why we miss them, and this is it. The tentative putt is the reason - the putt influenced by fear. The more vital the putt, the worse we become and the miss is on the right.

The mirror image of this is the pull or "drag" as it is more commonly known. "Oh dear, I've dragged it left" some people say ~ or words to that effect. They come across the line with a close faced putter.

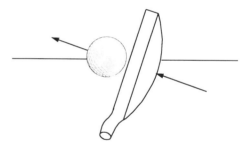

Figure 51

7. Hitting out of the toe or the heel of the putter. (figure 52)

To receive full force all putts must be hit from the sweet spot of the putter. The further you get away from this point the more the putter head will twist about it's centre of gravity. I know you will have seen some players line up with the toe of their putter, this is to compensate for a loop in their swing.

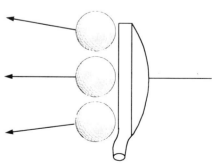

Figure 52

From the trials I have made, I have deduced one or two very important rules; rules which will bring more reliability into your game. Perhaps it would be pertinent to say that all golfers and not just beginners should follow these rules.

a.   Stand square or slightly open to the line of the putt. Whichever method suits you best in order for you to see the intended line.

b.   Hold your putter with your chosen grip. The nearer it is to the conventional the better. Don't just hold the club, "feel" the club, and this is best done without wearing a glove.

c.   Take the putter back as near to the line of the putt as you can, but not too far. Short distances for short putts and longer distances for the longer ones.

d.   On the forward swing the blade must return to square. If you swing slightly inside or outside the line, provided that the blade is square the putt will go in. There will be a slight error but a tolerable one.

e.   Hit the ball on the upswing to make sure there is no downwards force applied to the ball.

f.   Make sure you practise hitting the ball with the sweet spot of your putter. Find out where it is and if the manufacturer did not mark the spot, then mark it yourself.

g.   This is the last and perhaps most important rule of all. All putters must have a certain amount of loft. Only a few degrees but it is absolutely necessary. The putter can then be placed on the ground with its toe in the air, and this in effect closes the face slightly (figure 53). This solves two problems:

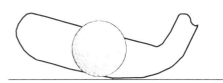

Figure 53

1.   If fear does get to you when you have a pressure putt, then the tentative putt will be corrected. This is because, when the toe is in the air, the putter blade is actually sightly closed even though it appears optically square. Try it out and see for yourself.

2.   On longer putts there is a tremendous force which acts on the club head and tries to open it. Raising the toe will again compensate for what has been calculated to be a 100 lb force on a 10 yard putt.

        Putting is the other half of the game. If you are good then you are a winner, if you are not then maybe some of my tips will help.

NINE

Fitness is a Must

There are many reasons why general fitness is invaluable to the golfer. Some are obvious, others not so obvious but all have some influence on the way you perform. Do you remember the time, when your legs told you how tired they were long before the end of the round? Unfortunately the tiredness you get in your legs does not stay there, it runs all the way up to your brain. When you get into a state of tiredness golf becomes a chore. Putts are not given enough care and attention, yardages do not seem to matter any more, and you cannot wait to "get in". If you were able to count how many times this situation has ruined your card, then you would certainly be persuaded to improve on your fitness.

Fitness for golf is essential and of more importance to the senior golfer than the younger player. Torn muscles and bad backs etc. take so much longer to heal as we get older. Muscle problems in the young take around three weeks to recover, as the years progress they can take months. Remember my fitness principle, "We must keep fit to play golf" and not "Play golf to keep fit". Perhaps we can go further than this and say, "We must keep fit so that we can play golf".

As a young professional and through most of my years on the European Tour I enjoyed running. I ran for one hour twice a week whether I was at home or away on Tour. Most golfers do not take fitness this seriously, but they should do something to keep their mind and body in good shape. Of course I don't run now, but I do keep as fit as I can and I never hit golf balls before warming up.

Now I am not going to suggest a training schedule for senior golfers that is anything like one designed for young athletes. Keeping fit has to be within our capability, both in the physical sense and in the time we have available. Whatever we do in life, we like it to be interesting and manageable. If it is not, then we very quickly lose any initial enthusiasm. We all follow active lives and if we are to introduce a fitness routine to golf then it has to fit in with our normal habits.

Away from golf, general fitness can be improved without adding extra things into a busy life style. The main thing to improve is your stamina because when you are "out of puff" you cannot hit golf balls. Everyone walks somewhere during the day and my advice is to walk at a faster rate. It is not necessary to run just walk faster than normal. When you walk up slopes take longer strides and two steps at a time when going up stairs. I am wisely informed that to raise your heart rate for short periods of time each day is a very healthy thing to do.

My personal fitness training at golf is simple. I do stretching exercises for ten minutes and then hit practise balls for anything up to half an hour. This is both a warming-up exercise and a check on how far the ball is flying. A ball will travel different distances on different days according to the weather conditions and this is important information. Jumping and running on the spot are also good for warming-up. On a cold day this should be done to slightly raise your heart rate before you stretch.

To start with, and to be on the safe side, I do my stretching exercises gently and slowly and count to 5 during each one. After each exercise "shake" yourself loose.

The stretching exercises used prior to playing, should also be used when you are out on the course. Waiting time can be utilised this way and can be worked into your pre-shot routine. Keeping your body supple during play adds to your competitive spirit and assists with your rhythm and timing.

We often read of the forces applied to the ball and forces to bend shafts, but have you ever considered the forces applied to you. When you swing a golf club, you can generate forces to the ball of up to 2000 Kgms - (2 tons). In doing this, the forces which pull you about are centrifugal forces. These are generated by the weight of the club head and are up to 50 Kgms (1 cwt) at the time of impact. This is like having to support a sack of potatoes on your shoulders at the time you hit the ball. If you do not brace yourself to support this force you will find it very difficult to remain in balance.

Swinging a golf club is not something to be casual about. You can injure yourself so easily if your body is not prepared to absorb the large forces generated during the swing. It is in your interest to do something about it.

EXERCISES BEFORE PLAY

1.   Stand tall, raise your arms above your head and stretch to touch the sky.

2.   Release the stretch by lowering your arms until they are by your sides.

3a.   Stand with your legs apart and move your body to the right to stretch your left side.

3b.   Move to the left to work your right side.

4a.   Place one foot in front of the other and keeping both feet on the ground, gently move your body forwards to be in line with your front foot. Do this for both legs.

4b.   Right leg stretch.

5a.   Stand with your feet shoulder width apart, put your hands on your hips and move your elbows as far forwards as they will go. Release to start position.

5b.   Stretch the upper back and shoulder muscles.

6.   Stand with your feet shoulder width apart, put your hands behind your head and move your elbows as far back as possible. Release to start position.

Having completed these exercises two or three times, I take a sand iron from the bag and practise the full swing - very slowly at first and never faster than a normal swing action. I then proceed to hit golf balls. A few short pitches with the sand iron and then full shots, working through the set with the even numbered clubs.

TEN

Technology and Equipment

To swing a golf club correctly commands an amazing sense of balance and coordination. In order for you to understand your input to this amazing feat, it is important that you know how your equipment works.

In golf it really does help to use "tools" to suit your ability. We tend to want to use the same clubs as the big stars of the game, but let's be sensible. If we all had the talent of players like Jack Nicklaus and Arnold Palmer, then we could use the same clubs (figures 54 + 55). We must be realistic when choosing our clubs and take advantage of modern technology. If we don't choose wisely then we soon know about it. Many golfers who change their clubs have to go through a lengthy new learning process which sometimes takes months.

More and more players are using cavity-back clubs. Forged blades are becoming a thing of the past and I can't remember when it was that I sold the last set. As you know I play cavity back clubs and have done for the past 19 years. In fact, the last time I played blades was in July 1977 in The Open at Turnberry. This was the year when Tom Watson beat Jack Nicklaus in a play off.

Very talented players hit the ball from the same spot on their clubs. Most golfers don't, and so find extra hitting area very useful. Cavity back clubs offer this facility and we should take advantage of it. Sweet spots which are larger actually offer two advantages. One is that off-centre hits cause less twisting of the club during the impact process and therefore hit the ball straighter and two, because less force is absorbed by the twisting motion, you will hit the ball further. Sweet spots on this type of club are in, or near to, the middle of the face. In blade clubs they are nearer to the heel and close to shank land. To many golfers this is good reason itself to play cavity back clubs.

Sweet spots are also very important in putters. You should find out where it is on your putter and mark its position. If you then make two other marks, 1/2 inch either side, this is the working area. The rest is cosmetic and is rarely used by the professional. The reason is obvious, a ball hit away from this area will come up short because some of the applied force is absorbed in twisting the putter. To ensure consistency of distance take more care to impact the ball in the hitting area.

Hollow metal woods - I think they will always be called woods - give the same advantage. They offer larger sweet spots but do beware of the bigger heads. You may block every thing out to the right if the head is too heavy.

Figure 54 Arnold Palmer and I take full advantage of modern technology.

Woods are now made of various materials. You can still buy wooden headed clubs which have plastic face inserts. Metal heads did not have face inserts until recently when carbon fibre was used to offer less spin to the ball than steel. This is fine for the driver where we need run on the ball but less of a requirement in the shorter clubs when we are looking to stop the ball.

Spin is generated during the period of time that the ball is in contact with the club face. This time period is 1/2 of one thousandth of one second. Not a large amount of time so the spin mechanism has to be very powerful. When we discuss spin we do tend to concentrate on back spin. We should also consider top spin and side spin because they are equally important.

The spin generated by players like Nick Faldo has been calculated to be in the order of 8,000 rpm from a wedge shot and there are several factors involved in spin (figure 56). These are, club head speed, friction, loft, shaft flex, grooves and the centre of gravity of the club head. Perhaps the main factor being the impact position on the club face.

A ball hit low in the club face will acquire the most back spin. If it is hit high in the club face it will obtain less back spin and this is why we tee up high when using the driver. A ball hit out of the toe will have draw spin and the one out of the heel will fade. These are not just facts they are very useful at times. If out of bounds on the left bothers you then hit the ball out of the heel of the club. Alternatively, if you don't want to hit the ball right then make use of the toe area of the club. In both cases you will loose distance but it is better than losing shots and balls.

Figure 55 Arnold Palmer.

Figure 56 Nick Faldo.

The ball construction also has a part to play and some spin much faster than others. I must remind you that balls which are advertised to fly further, spin less and are therefore more difficult to stop on the greens. You really do have to decide what you want from a ball.

Shafts

Back in the beginning, shafts were made of wood. Blackthorn and Hickory were the two main woods and were tapered to suit the grip and the flex. They were somewhat smaller in diameter at the tip end where they entered the head and large enough at the grip end to take a thin leather wrapping. The grip end was about an inch or so in diameter and individually designed to suit the player. Then came the steel shaft and this was made to model the wooden one with one deliberate change. It is manufactured to be the same weight per unit length, thus its centre of gravity is half way down the shaft.

Now we have fibre glass reinforced plastics with carbon and boron fibres. There are plastic shafts, light weight metal shafts and goodness knows what next, but what are we looking for in a shaft? Its job is to present the club head to the ball in the correct manner and this is different for different players. Flexes vary according to the way we swing the club and it would be perfect if the shaft were straight at impact. For some top players this may be so but for most players it is not. The shaft, if we consider the swing plane, is c-shaped at impact. This means that the club has taken up a shape which gives the club a dynamic loft.

Players who have difficulty getting the ball airborne should therefore use more flexible shafts. Those who hit the ball too high should use a stiffer shaft, but don't mistake high trajectory shots for skied shots. These are caused if the flat which is made on the ball at impact is partly overlapping the top of the club face. This shot goes seriously skywards, just as the ones which wrap around the toe or the heel, go seriously sideways. We also know that the ones we "top" hit the ground just in front of our feet.

As our years progress it may also be necessary to use a driver with a little more loft - I have to. Drivers can have as little a 7 degrees of loft, perhaps 12 degrees is more suitable for the senior player.

Kick points in shafts also help overcome the same problems. A kick point is where the bend in the shaft is at the smallest radius. If this is lower than normal it is said to have a low kick point and conversely a higher kick point.

Torque is a term often used when describing shafts. It would be easier to understand if we talked about twist, particularly resistance to twist. In steel shafts flex and twist change together. That is, a flexible shaft has less resistance to twist. This is not necessarily so with the carbon fibre type of shaft, because it can be made to be flexible and yet have good resistance to twist.

These new developments in shaft design and manufacture can be of advantage to many players. The shock waves which travel up a carbon fibre shaft are softer than through steel and many golfers who have hand and wrist problems would be advised to try them out. But please don't go for heavier heads just because the shaft is lighter. You will only find the club more difficult to play. Yes, you may hit the odd one longer, though not necessarily in the right direction.

Grips

Grips are much more important than many golfers imagine. They connect you, via the shaft to the club head. How you present the grip at the time of impact has an important part to play in shot making. Perhaps you have never thought of it this way, but you should be able to see why I mention it. If the orientation of the grip is wrong at impact then the head is too.

Another feature of the grip is that it is tapered from top to bottom. This is to help you resist the centrifugal force which acts down and along the shaft throughout the swing. It is important to keep your grips dry to stop your club slipping through your hands and of course to stop it twisting. So take good care of your grips by washing them regularly with soapy water and give them the occasional rub down with sand paper.

Grip diameter should vary according to the size of a player's hands. In general the standard size is OK, but if you have large or small hands then see your pro for advice. Various sized grips are available but check that they are the same weight as standard grips. Mens' grips are normally 50 grammes and a change in weight may change your swing.

The Golf Ball

Do you play with a brand of ball to suit your game or your pocket?

The golf ball we play with has changed quite dramatically over the years. It was first made of a leather case, stitched in a similar way to that of a hockey ball, and stuffed with feathers. Enough feathers in fact to fill a top hat over its brim. It was called the feathery and right at the very beginning it was found to play longer when the surface became roughened by wear.

When the "gutta-percha" ball appeared on the market it had a patterned surface to give it better flight characteristics. These patterns have since changed and varied so considerably that the top manufactures have put together some of the old balls and mounted them in display boxes. One of these is now on show in The Belfry Hotel and makes very interesting viewing.

Just before impact.

At impact.

Just after impact.

The patterns on the earlier balls were pimples and not the dimples we know today. In the time since the pimples all manner of ways have been employed to roughen the surface. Every conceivable shape has been tried but the dimple with its ease of cleaning has survived the longest time.

The dimples vary both in size and in the way they are arranged. But it's the overall construction of the ball which has seen the most important change in recent years. There is now a two piece ball as well as the three piece ball and golfers have their own reasons for choosing between the two.

Professionals still like the three piece construction because it gives a better performance around the greens. It "checks up" better and as professionals hit the ball a long way, they can then confidently pitch the ball onto the greens.

Many amateurs find the two piece ball to be better, because of the same reason for which the professionals reject it. It travels well after it lands and will run giving the extra distance demanded by the shorter hitting player.

The three piece ball, which is more inclined to "bite" when landing on the green, has been around for many years. It is constructed by winding rubber band elastic around a hard or soft core. The "cores" are frozen to make the winding operation possible and the outer case, made of various materials such as balata or surlyn is fitted over the rubber winding. Finally, the balls are painted named and packed.

The two piece ball, which is now very widely used, has one core. During manufacture it is frozen and then ground to make sure it is perfectly round. This also makes sure that it is well balanced. Finally the outer case is fitted and painted.

The backspin we all talk about in golf is imparted into the ball whilst it is in contact with the club. When the ball lands on hard ground, only some of the spin is absorbed by the ground, the rest goes into reverse and the ball rolls on. If the greens or the fairways are receptive, then the ball will retain part of its backspin and stop on the second contact with the ground. The more spin you can give to the ball the better chance it has to stop. Obviously the wedge is the best club to do the job, and even then a good clean hit is required.

The golf ball takes a terrific bashing from all golfers, and has to be very resilient. The bashing in the early days of the feathery made the "thinkers" of that time ask why this roughness gave the ball more lift.

One person who looked into the flight of balls in those early days was a German Professor named Magnus. His work lead to the discovery of what was later called the Magnus Effect, and it is of great use to golfers.

He found that when a ball is spinning through the air, it creates a low pressure area which gives it lift. This gives the ball more height and also has an effect on distance when there is a cross wind.

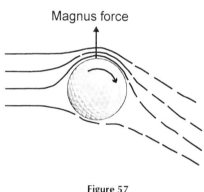

Magnus force

Figure 57

When playing in a cross wind, a golfer is always tempted to try and curve the ball into the wind. This way he expects to get the best results. It may help if he is looking to keep the ball on the short grass, but if he is looking for distance he must spin the ball with the wind direction.

If you look at figure 57 you will see that when a ball is spinning in a cross wind, it will pull the air round its surface. This, in turn, tightens the flow of air and creates a low pressure area at the front of the ball. To use this information to our advantage we fade the ball on a left to right wind to get greater distance. For the same reason, a ball spinning from right to left on a right to left wind will go further.

Knowing more about how your golf ball behaves is an added advantage. Make sure it is of good quality and cleaned at every opportunity.

What to Wear

Lets start with shoes and work upwards. Golf shoes more than anything else are an aid to balance. For this reason spikes are better than rubber dimples. You do not need so many spikes and this means that they are almost self cleaning. I know that there will always be some grass wrapped around the spikes but there is less chance of the whole sole becoming clogged with mud.

Balance plays a big part in the game and you must take every measure to attain it. Look at your shoes and see if any studs are missing and if they are starting to wear down, get them replaced. When I am in my shop, I am sometimes asked to replace a set of studs. I do this with pleasure, not just for the business, but because I respect a golfer who cares about his golf.

I always have more than one pair of shoes wherever I travel. If I have to play extra holes, it is so much nicer to go out again in warm dry shoes. This goes for all of your clothes, you have to be comfortable at this game. There is nothing worse than being wet through even in the summer - to have extra socks and shoes is a sensible move. The same applies to gloves and do take care of them.

Today, golfers take more care with how they dress for the course. I approve of this because golf itself is a caring game in every respect. Care in club selection, care in decision making and so on. These are essential if you want to play well. Looking good makes you feel good and leads to better golf.

Hats and visors are very useful to golfers. There are obvious reasons why we wear them such as protection from sun and rain. Hats also keep you warm on cold days but there is a much more important reason. Where there are lots of spectators there will always be someone who moves and distracts you when you are on your backswing. We all know that it is difficult to stop once we have started the swing and this usually results in a bad shot. It can "wind you up" and then you can make yourself look silly. None of this will have the chance to happen if you use the brim of a hat or a visor to hide behind. This is another part of the care and preparation exercise.

Ride or Carry

There are many seniors who still play and enjoy the game after they have retired from business. Some clubs have more older members than others and this is perhaps due to the walk-ability of the course. There are courses which are more suitable for hill climbers, but even then, older golfers will find a way to solve the problem. No problem is too difficult for the ardent golfer. He/she thrives on such conditions because golf is a problem solving game. All of the older golfers that I know have one thing in common, they are still ambitious and want to get to grips with their game.

When we become senior seniors we have to make provision to remain involved in the game. I suppose we could resort to spectating but although this is very interesting, we would be somewhat bored during the winter months. Personally I get great pleasure from watching the Golden Oldies from the US tour start the proceedings at The Masters and The Open. What a delight it was to see Gene Sarazen at the age of 80, hole in one at the Postage Stamp at Royal Troon in 1991. But just like you I get my greatest pleasure from playing and will continue to do so whilst my health allows me to - perhaps then I shall become a professional spectator.

The caddy car is a good friend of the senior golfer.

There are certain requirements which get more important as we become older. Help with walking and carrying are just two, both are more easily overcome these days than they were years ago. It's not so long ago that we had to employ a caddy to help with the bag. However, this facility is not so readily available today through the availability of motorised trollies and ride on caddy cars.

The main failing from these new machines is that they do not offer advice and yardages. These have to be decided upon by studying yardage charts which is not quite the same. It is not too difficult to work out club selection from chart information, but what about line? The experienced caddy will always be better at making these decisions. There is one plus though, you can drink and drive the modern caddy car if you like to take your flask with you.

I carry when I can for fitness reasons. I feel that when I practice on the course to hone up my ability to read distances and putts, it is just as important to remember my fitness. Being fit to play 18 holes is not enough in my business. I need to be strong going up the last to cope with the pressure situation. Tiredness at this time in professional golf could prove to be expensive.

Of course not all golfers can afford such luxuries as carts and cars. They cost an arm and a leg and are not always a good solution to the problem. Sometimes it's better to use a pencil bag and carry less clubs (figure 58). If this is the case which clubs should you carry?

Well the putter for a start and perhaps a jigger (figure 59). The jigger is also known as a chipper and I don't know if it was designed in the Jigger Inn by the side of the 17th on the Old Course at St Andrews (figure 60). Maybe those old golfers, who could not always take a dram or two before play to settle the nerves, might well have designed the club to solve their chipping problems.

Figure 58 Pencil bag.

Figure 59 A jigger.

Now I thought that this was an interesting theory, but on my last visit to St Andrews I was told a better story. In fact my first theory is back to front. The Jigger Inn was named after the club. The Inn as you may know was originally the Railway Station Masters House and is named the Jigger Inn because it is so close to the green of the famous road hole.

Back with our clubs, we will need clubs for getting out of trouble, like the sand iron and the nine iron. You may say a wedge in preference to the nine, but I would opt for the nine because it will cover more distance when it is needed.

Chipping and pitching can be played quite successfully with the sand iron. This club has a sole designed to bounce off sand and will therefore be more forgiving if you hit behind the ball when playing from the fairway. You may find that you might thin the shot now and again because of the bounce, but that is far more acceptable than "muffing" the shot. Thinning a shot by the way, is hitting the ball with the front bottom edge of the club face and the ball then runs along the ground. Of course this can be eradicated when chipping if you do decide to carry a jigger.

Every golfer carries a seven iron. There is something very special about this club and all golfers can use it. It's everyone's favourite iron and when the swing is not performing as well as we would like, the seven iron is the saving club. If ever we are faced with a shot where we have to play short of a hazard or if we simply cannot cover the distance, then the seven iron is a good club to use.

Figure 60 The Jigger Inn.

We often find that control shots are required. It may be that we have to deal with a hazard or need a better line into a green. The seven iron will do the job admirably; playing your favourite club will give you the confidence to play this type of shot with some authority.

A five iron would also be a good club to carry. This is a distance iron and should perhaps be the longest iron in the bag. A one, two, three or four may be OK if you can use them, but from my experience of giving lessons and playing with members, many golfers of all ages hit the ball the same or very similar distances with any of these clubs. It therefore makes sense to only carry a five iron because at all levels of golf, consistency is the prime requirement.

For more distance we should carry woods. These are of particular importance when playing from the semi rough.They move and flatten the grass away from the face of the club instead of cutting the grass. This gives less resistance to club head speed and therefore greater distance to the shot.

The five wood particularly is a good club for this job and gets the ball airborne very quickly. A seven wood may be even better for some golfers so that the ball clears the grass even quicker. We are all aware of the fact that the grass may reduce club head speed, but grass interference after club head contact, just smothers the ball. Whether the ball is in the rough, in a hazard or any poor lie, the first objective is to get the ball out into a more playable position.

Getting the ball airborne is not just a problem from the rough. To get a ball onto an acceptable trajectory requires both club head speed and loft. As we become less able to provide the former then we must use the latter.

A ball flying at an angle of 45 degrees will give the most carry. On wet days this will provide more distance, although it is less important for distance on dry days. Even so, it is important to get the ball in the air and the loft required is provided by both the club head and the shaft flex. As I stated earlier, when the club makes contact with the ball, the shaft is bent forward. So the more flexible the shaft, the more the dynamic loft and the easier it is to get the ball up and on its way.

Under the same rule, tee shots would be better played with a three or even a five wood. A flexible shaft with good resistance to twist will do the best job and these qualities are best offered in composite shafts. The quality and reliability of modern fibre composite shafts will do the job and again, as I mentioned earlier, have the added advantage of being less arduous on the hands and wrists than steel shafts.

So if we total up the minimum amount of clubs needed to do a good job it's eight. Three wood, five wood, five iron, seven iron, nine iron, sand wedge, jigger and putter.

I do not believe that there are any other special requirements for the golden oldies of any golf club. You do not need me to tell you things like the quickest route back to the club house for a pot of tea or another dram.

GOLF IS A WAY OF LIFE

Everyone who plays this great game of golf understands the pleasure it gives to all peoples around the world. How would we meet so many nice people if we did not play golf? We talk it, eat it and sleep it and if we are not doing that then we are planning the next outing.

Make sure that your planning arrangements are complete. To look after your equipment and to practise wisely is only part of it. You should take advantage of modern technology and use equipment to suit your age and ability. You should also remember that your scores will reflect the amount of care and effort which you are prepared to put into the game. All of this is very worthwhile because, as we all know, a good round of golf makes any problems in life seem much less important.

To be playing golf is a privilege. Perhaps to me it's more than that - I'm lucky to still be playing. I will make sure from now on that I enjoy everything the game has to offer me, and so should you.

Good golfing and best wishes